PU PU HOT POT

AFRICA

ASIA

HINDENBURGER
Flame Broiled

Burger Combo
$4.99

Fresh Fruit Smoothies

ANGKOR WHAT

abrakebabra

Australia

a little girl typhoon

PU PU HOT POT

The World's Best Restaurant Names

BEN BRUSEY

St. Martin's Griffin ❧ New York

A Note of Thanks: I would like to thank Patty Chen for her contribution of the name PuPu Hot Pot for this book. The name was created when Patty and her father could not decide whether to open a hot pot restaurant or sell pupu platters. The name is a combination of the two. *The Boston Globe* said that the name was "easy to remember and hard to forget." *The Boston Phoenix* wrote "Lousy Name, Great Food." Now, it is hard to find anyone who has lived in Cambridge who does not recognize Patty and her family's restaurant. In her immortal words, "PuPu Hot Pot, may I help you?"

PU PU HOT POT. Copyright © 2012 by Ben Brusey. All rights reserved. Printed in China. For more information, address St. Martin's Press, 175 Fifth Avenue, New York, N.Y. 10010

www.stmartins.com

ISBN 978-1-250-03454-0 (trade paperback)
ISBN 978-1-250-03455-7 (e-book)

St. Martin's Griffin books may be purchased for educational, business, or promotional use. For information on bulk purchases, please contact Macmillan Corporate and Premium Sales Department at 1-800-221-7945 extension 5442 or write specialmarkets@macmillan.com

First published in Great Britain by Viking, an imprint of Penguin Books

First U.S. Edition: June 2013

10 9 8 7 6 5 4 3 2 1

PU PU HOT POT

But no bits & bobs.

One hot mess…

There's something in the eggnog.

Kebabs especially for you. Or to share with neighbors.

You know what they say about restaurants with big plates…

2-for-1 on Back to Black label vodka.

Cod is a DJ.

Sister store to Sell Fridges.

Spice that rubs you up the wrong way.

PHẬT PHÚC
NOODLE BAR

Authentic Vietnamese
Noodle Soup

"Phật Phúc" translates as "Happy Buddha." Seriously.

Eating with the fishes.

You'll be bowled over.

Piggie Piggie Piggie, can't you see
Sometimes your baps just hypnotize me.

Get your vines off me, you damned dirty grapes!

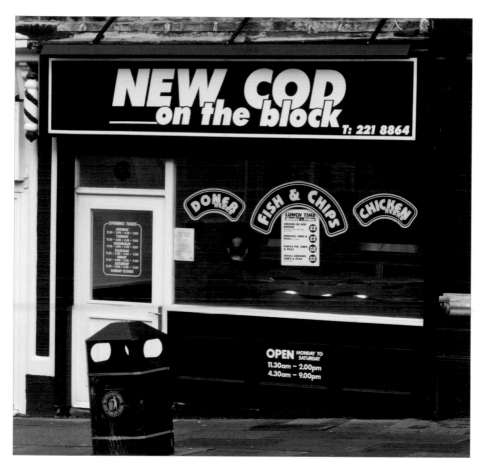

Previously "The Gill Next Door."

Not Vajayjay.

Tired mochas,
washed-up
espressos.

The best sausage sandwiches around.

Getting to know you! Over Pad Thai.

Come for the steak, stay for the company.

Fish are food, not friends.

Pull the Doner from the hat.

Full of fresh aromas.

That's the last time I'll eat there!

Knock knock! Who's there? Falafel. Falafel who? Falafel off his bike and hurt his knee!

"Food with passion to get your pulse racing." — *XXX Review*

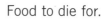

Food to die for.

"Darkly atmospheric."

—Anonymous customer review

"Call me Fishmael."

Enter the belly of the beast.

UN peacekeepers were sent in to relieve Americano drinkers.

The plaice for Motown flavor.

Like this!

Easy on the ketchup, heavy on the puns.

The ultimate knock-off cuisine.

Includes the classic hit dish Bohemian Anchovy.

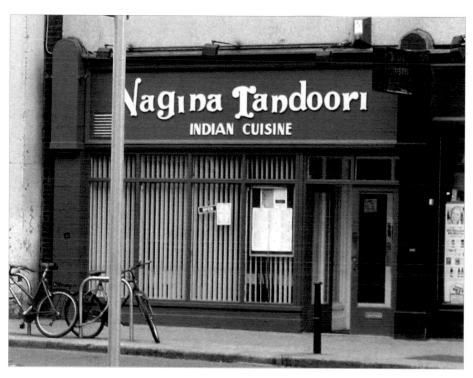

Warning: Hot spice. Not for pussies.

Couples welcome,
of all ages.

Dine with your boots on.

But treat her right.

Not Number One.

Vietnamese has never been so gangsta.

A chance eating.

Flame grilled and disastrously good.

Prepared by hand.

You'll never share a table again (because they have none).

It's been emotional…

Avoid the iceberg lettuce.

Made fresh daily.

Chef's tip: quit lookin' at him funny.

The perfect comfort break.

Can we eat it? YES WE CAN!

The Lord grills in mysterious ways.

Put fire in your belly.

Hot dog tastes great.

Chicks with attitude.

Your dinner.

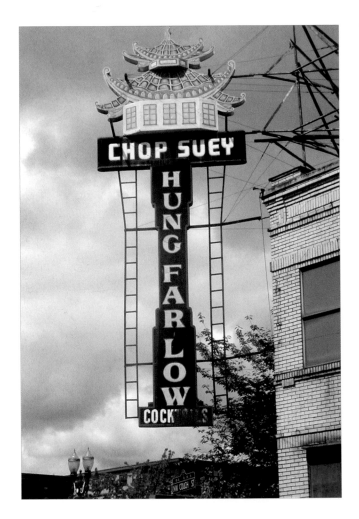

The biggest
dumplings around.

Eat here and you'll never grow up.

Serves only 100% Chinese pork.

Something smells fishy in here.

And the Best Hot Dog goes to…you. And you. And you…

You won't know what hit you.

Stuff your poker face.

Hot dogs you can believe in.

East fast (food), die young.

Managing customer
expectation since
1972.

Sushi to warm your heart.

A latte energy in the morning.

You'll keep coming back for more…

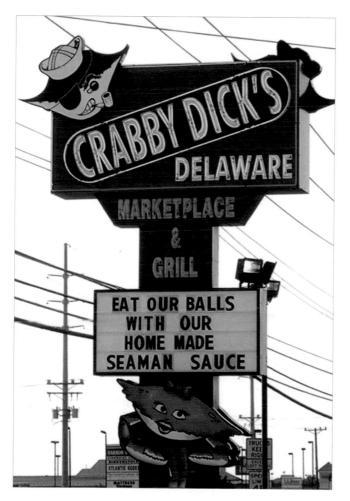

Winner of the 2012 Good Taste Awards.

Margaritas with morals.

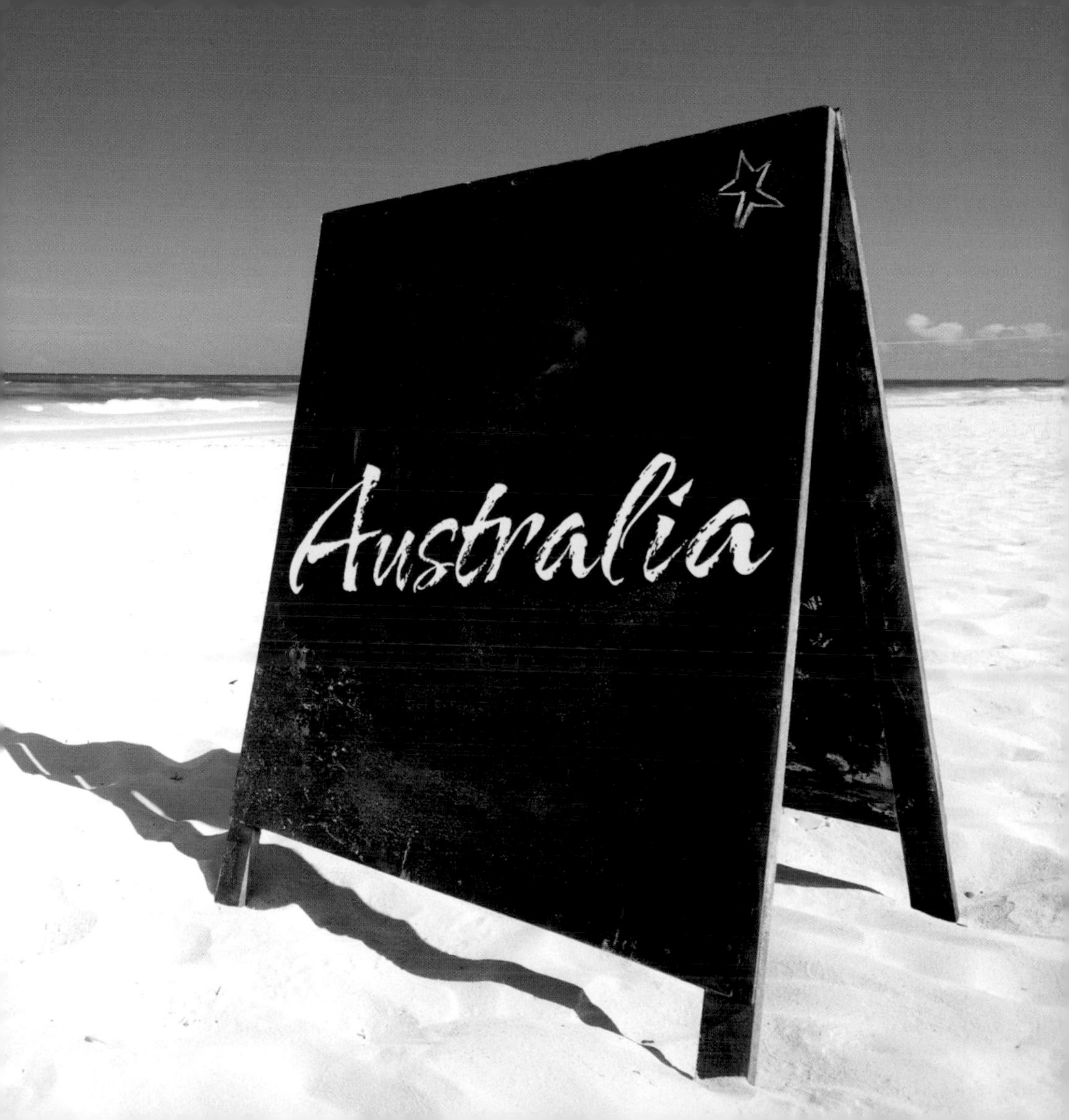
Australia

Children must be supervised by an adult (at all times).

Medium, rare, or extinct.

Brides-to-go.

Green Curry: the perfect date bait.

A great gastro pub.

High-minded dining.

So that's where Osama was hiding…

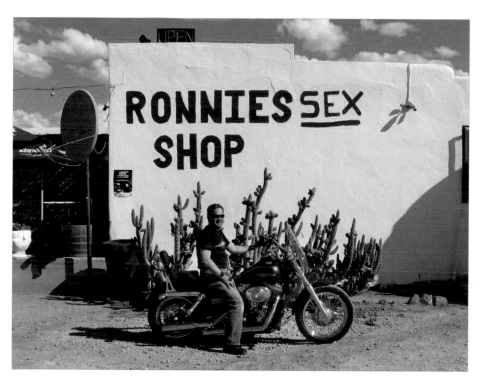

The birds and the bees—over lunch.

A Leap of Faith (into a frying vat).

Mayor of London HQ.

King of Mince.

Grand Tofu Master of the Universe.

Don't expect them to get your order right.

If it's good enough for Goldilocks, it's good enough for you.

Full address still pending.

Now with plumbing at each table.

You won't feel, or taste, a thing.

So why not give it to him? (He'll taste better).

Aromatic, full-flavored blends also available.

Food with a happy ending.

Inewitable gweat food.

Prices that won't ruin you.

Do NOT upset the waitress.

Even the gravy exudes charisma.

When the weight of the world is just too much…

Warning: food may contain traces of teenage boy.

牛丼 | かつ丼

BEEF BAWL

Eye-wateringly good food.

"Big Yac and fries, please."

Raised to be dinner.

The Bucks stop here.

Breakfast? Whatever…

Where pigs go "moo."

You bring the beef, I'll bring the swine.

Always wash your hands AFTER you eat.

All your needs for a good night out.

Don't miss the glazed donuts.

ACKNOWLEDGMENTS

I would like to thank the following people for providing photographs. Without you, this book would not have been possible.

Paul Little, Jamie Brusey, David Brusey, Caroline Brusey, Jamie Palmer, Chris Stoddart, Christian Cable, Johnnie Packington, Tom Page-Phillips, Thomas Guest, Ross MacPherson, Kim Bülow Bonfils, Michael Shepherd, Doug Newton, Gill Theaker, Jeremy Markowitz, Mark Norman Francis, Steve Mannion, Keely Richardson, Heather Rai, Bill Kennedy, Fred McElwaine, Kristina Thimm, Patrick Smith (www.askthepilot.com), Anton Zafereo, Vinayak Hegde, Erhan Erdoğan, Jesse Russell, Esmond Yau, Stephen Wray, Andrew Nguyen, Patrick Tanguay, Martyn Weir, Matt Richardson, Dianne Krone, Chris Bullneck, Jeremy Schultz, Victor Tate Photography, www.asaltandbattery.com, David Cory, Nelson Wan, Lance Eckels, Ahmet Ziyaeddin, Catherine Ling, Elliot Cheung, Jeremiah Allen, Jerry Abstract, Mark K, Renee Huang, Saul Blumenthal, Linus Lee, Tony Singh, Turner Wright, Elise Bernard, Jon Racasa, Bruce Fingerhood, Rachael McCurdy, Henry Ho, Patricia S. Greenstein, Daphne Chong, David Myers, David Mallozzi, Eric Steuer, Becky Houtman, Michael Bruchas, Sarah Jae-Jones, Stephanie Steele, Bill Trenwith, scottamus on Flickr, Sam Koronczyk, Nari Clarke, Ashok Hariharan, Dan Rosenberg, Danie van der Merwe, Karon Liu, William James Tychonievich, Thomas Scherber, Will Gee, Aram Armstrong, Robert Rabinowitz, Will Burns, Troy Parsons, Stefan I., Trishan Panch (www.hybridvigour.net), Carianne Carleo-Evangelist, David Lewinnek, Nathan Wales, Camemberu.com,

Peter Cuce, Nils Trebing, Emily S. Lee, D. Müller, Marie McClellan, Cheng "hellaOAKLAND," Mohamed Salim, Tanya Procyshyn, Jeremiah Roth, Sarah Blythe, Tom Bromwich, Marissa Chen, Joe Brooke, Lily Faber, Lesley Faber, Penguin Press crew, David Walker, Nick Hill, Nicky Palmer, Mark Ollard, Matt Clacher, Jess Kim, Lija Kresowaty, Caroline Craig, Jo Davy (www.davy.co.uk), Paul Little.

I am greatly indebted to the brilliant Charlotte Humphery, who superbly assembled the book, and spent many an afternoon banging her head against her desk helping to come up with captions. To Gesche Ipsen, Marissa Chen, Kyle McEnery and everyone at Penguin, thank you for your help and suggestions. I am very grateful also to Keith Taylor, Hannah Bradbury, Gill Heeley, and Andrew Smith for expertly steering, producing, and designing the book. Most of all, I would like to thank Lily Faber: your humor, kindness, and patience knows no bounds—especially when we were walking around London together taking pictures of restaurants like "Vijay" in subzero temperatures.